What Do I look Like?

By EmauniJ and Roz Manley
Illustrated by LJ Thomas

Written by: EmauniJ and Roz Manley
Illustrations By: LJ Thomas

ISBN: 978-1985571778

Printed in the United States of America

Cover Illustration LJ Thomas of Asoral
Graphics by LJ Thomas and Freepik
Book design, editing and production by LJ Thomas,
www.asoral.com
Author photographed by various photographers

To learn more about EmauniJ or for questions please reach out to CDD MGMT. Email:chrisdeldavismgmt@gmail.com
Website: www.valenciasworld7.info
Office Number 1-877-732-8261

Don't forget to follow EmauniJ on Instagram
@Emaunijmanley

Dream   Big

♡ Emaunij

Dedication

To the first man I ever loved, my daddy Albert Manley, Jr. Thank you for reading to me every night. It's because of you that I love to read. I love spending time with you. Our bond is beautiful. You and my brothers are perfect examples of a few good men. Thank you for letting me know I'm Smart and I'm Beautiful.

Love your Princess Emauni

EmauniJ

A daughter needs a dad to be the standard against which she will judge all men.

EmauniJ

EmauniJ and all of her loving brothers.

What do I look like in the morning
when I wake up?

When I'm brushing my teeth in the mirror what do I look like?

What do I look like when I'm dressing for the day?

Or when Mommy is doing my hair

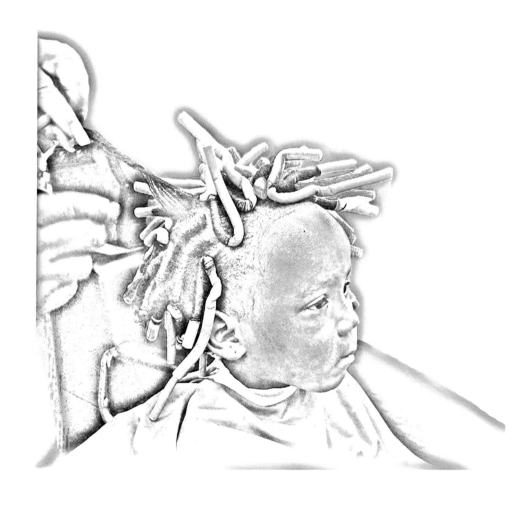

What do I look like when I go outside to play?

What do I look like when I've had a bad day?

Or when it's a rainy gloomy day.

No matter my hairstyle.

Or the time of day.

No matter the sunshine or huge clouds that get in my way.

What do I look like you ask?

I am fearfully and wonderfully made
and so are you.

About EmauniJ

Emauni J. Manley was born in Charles County, MD in August 2012. She is the youngest of her parent's 4 children and the only daughter. Emauni has a passion for reading, dancing, singing, modeling and fashion. Every morning Emauni looks in the mirror and tells herself "I'm smart and I'm beautiful. She says this often throughout the day. Her mother taught her to say this at a young age.

You can often times hear Emauni ask "What do I look like?" when she has a new outfit, hairstyle or when she wakes up in the morning. She started doing this on her own at the age of 2. She said this so much that her dad wrote it in her room over her mirror. He wanted her to know that no matter what, she is beautiful. Emauni is full of ideas. She always sees the best in everything and everyone. She strives hard in school and is loved by everyone she comes in contact with.

Every night Emauni says her prayers with her mom, afterwards her dad tucks her in and reads her a story. One day Emauni said she wanted to write a book so she could add it to her book collection. The next day she asked her parents to help her write a book and start her own clothing line and call it EmauniJ. EmauniJ was created on that day.

EmauniJ Collection